The Threefold Nature of Man

Volume 1 of the Spirit, Soul, and Body
Series

(Formerly titled: Man On Three Dimensions)

Kenneth E. Hagin

Unless otherwise indicated, all Scripture quotations in this volume are from the *King James Version* of the Bible.

Second Edition
First Printing 1996

ISBN 0-89276-032-X

In the U.S. write:
Kenneth Hagin Ministries
P.O. Box 50126
Tulsa, OK 74150-0126

In Canada write:
Kenneth Hagin Ministries
P.O. Box 335, Station D,
Etobicoke (Toronto), Ontario
Canada, M9A 4X3

Copyright © 1973 RHEMA Bible Church
AKA Kenneth Hagin Ministries, Inc.
All Rights Reserved
Printed in USA

The Faith Shield is a trademark of RHEMA Bible Church, AKA Kenneth Hagin Ministries, Inc., registered with the U.S. Patent and Trademark Office and therefore may not be duplicated.

Contents

The Spirit, Soul, and Body Series:

Volume 1 — *The Threefold Nature of Man*
Volume 2 — *The Human Spirit*

Chapter I

THE THREE-FOLD NATURE OF MAN

The study of man's three-fold nature — the spirit, soul, and body — is one which always intrigued me. I have sought earnestly to learn the difference between the three. It is easy enough to distinguish between the body and the other two. But it is sometimes difficult to distinguish between the spirit and the soul. Nothing but the Bible can do that. Misunderstanding on this subject abounds. Much error has been taught, even from the pulpit.

For years I studied the books used in various theological schools on the study of man in my search for the truth in this area. I studied the books taught by the Full Gospel Bible schools. I had the books used by the denomination which I had belonged to previously. But I found little satisfaction from all these. They were all based on the teachings of individuals and not on the Bible.

I talked to some of the most able Bible teachers in Full Gospel circles. I talked to some who had earned doctorate degrees in theology. It was surprising how little most of them knew on the subject of man's spirit, soul, and body.

Some have said to me, "I always thought the spirit and the soul were the same. I've always preached it that way." But I pointed out to them that they couldn't be the same. Otherwise why would the Bible say, "For the word of God is quick, and powerful, and sharper than any two-edged sword, piercing even to the dividing asunder of soul and spirit . . . ." (Heb. 4:12)? If they were the same, they could not be divided. If they were the same, Paul would not have said, ". . . I pray God your whole spirit and soul and body be preserved blameless unto the coming of our Lord Jesus Christ" (I Thess. 5:23).

It would be just as scriptural to say that the body and the soul are the same as it would be to say that the spirit and the soul are the same. In reality they are three very distinct things.

After much prayer and study over a long period of time I arrived at my conclusions on the three dimensions of man in this way. I knew without argument that with the physical body we contact the world. The body deals in the physical realm. No one will dispute that. Then, as I studied I saw that it is the spirit of man that contacts God, for God is a Spirit. Only a spirit could contact a spirit. The new birth is a rebirth of the human spirit, for Jesus told Nicodemus, ". . . . Ye must be born again" (John 3:7). Nicodemus, being natural, could only think naturally, so he said, "How can a man be born when he is old? can he enter the second time into his mother's womb, and be born?" Jesus answered, "That which is born of the flesh is flesh; and that which is born of the Spirit is spirit."

Then I decided I would go through the entire New Testament, seeing what Paul and the other apostles said on this subject. I found where Paul said in Romans 2:28-29, "For he is not a Jew, which is one outwardly; neither is that circumcision, which is outward in the flesh: But he is a Jew, which is one inwardly; and circumcision is that of the heart, in the spirit, and not in the letter; whose praise is not of men, but of God." Paul was saying here that the spirit is the heart.

Then in I Corinthians 14:14 we read, "For if I pray in an unknown tongue, my spirit prayeth . . . ." The Amplified Translation reads, "My spirit (by the Holy Spirit within me prays . . . ." In Verse 18 Paul said, "I thank my God, I speak with tongues more than ye all." Paul used the terms "my spirit" and "I" interchangeably.

Having seen that with the body we contact the physical realm and with the spirit we contact the spiritual realm, that left only the soul to locate. Since the body deals with the physical realm and the spirit deals with the spiritual realm, that left only one other realm that man is involved in — the mental realm. So with the soul we contact the intellectual realm. This is, of course, simplifying it in the extreme. As we go further in our study of this subject we shall delve into it more deeply. But here in this first chapter we are just laying the foundation.

Briefly, man's three-fold nature is this:

6

(1) Spirit — The dimension of man which deals with the spiritual realm. The part of man that knows God.

(2) Soul — The dimension of man which deals with the mental realm. Man's intellect. The sensibilities and will. The part that reasons and thinks.

(3) Body — The dimension of man which deals with the physical realm. The house in which we live.

I want you to begin thinking of yourself in a new light. Don't think of yourself as just a physical being. Think of yourself as a spirit being who possesses a soul and lives in a body.

Chapter II

MAN'S FIRST DIMENSION — THE SPIRIT

Man is a spirit who possesses a soul and lives in a body. Man's spirit is that part of him that knows God. He is in the same class with God because God is a Spirit and God made man to fellowship with Him. God made man for His own pleasure. Man is not an animal. In order to fellowship with God, man must be in the same category with God. Therefore, just as God is Spirit, so is man spirit.

By way of illustration let me ask, did you ever try to fellowship with an old cow? We can't fellowship with cows because they are in a different kingdom, a different class than we are. But we can fellowship with one another, and we can fellowship with God because we are the same type of being.

Jesus told the woman at the well in Samaria, "God is a Spirit: and they that worship him must worship him in spirit and in truth" (John 4:24). We cannot know God or touch Him physically. He is not a man. He is Spirit. We cannot communicate with God mentally, for He is a Spirit. But we can reach Him with our spirit, and it is through our spirit that we come to know God.

So we know that God is a Spirit. And yet God, who is a Spirit, took upon Himself a man's body. Jesus was God manifested in the flesh. "In the beginning was the Word, and the Word was with God, and the Word was God. The same was in the beginning with God. All things were made by him; and without him was not any thing made that was made . . . And the Word was made flesh, and dwelt among us . . . ." (John 1:1-3, 14).

When God took upon Himself human form, He was no less God than when He didn't have a body. Man, at physical death,

8

leaves his body. Yet he is no less man than he was when he had his body. We see this in Christ's account of Lazarus and the rich man at death (Luke 16:19-31).

In Paul's epistle to the church at Thessalonica we see a glimpse of man's three-fold nature. "And the very God of peace sanctify you wholly; and I pray God your whole spirit and soul and body be preserved blameless unto the coming of our Lord Jesus Christ" (I Thess. 5:23).

Another version translates this verse, "I pray God your whole spirit and soul and body be preserved entire, without blame, at the coming of the Lord Jesus Christ." This three-fold man is to be preserved "entire," without blame at the coming of the Lord. That will be a great day, for when the Lord comes, this whole man — spirit, soul, and body — will be preserved "entire."

We have a new spirit now, for our spirits are born of God. But we will have a new body "at the coming of the Lord Jesus Christ." We have a new life now, but we will have a new body then.

More than one Old Testament prophet prophesied concerning Israel that God would establish a new covenant with the house of Israel. This new covenant is the New Testament as we know it. Through the prophet Ezekiel God said, "A new heart also will I give you, and a new spirit will I put within you: and I will take away the stony heart out of your flesh, and I will give you an heart of flesh. And I will put my spirit within you, and cause you to walk in my statutes and ye shall keep my judgements, and do them" (Ezek. 36:26-27).

Ezekiel was prophesying concerning the new birth. When a man is born again, the spirit (which is the real man) is born again and the old man is gone. The old hard, stony heart is gone. He is a new creature, as Paul said in II Corinthians 5:17, "Therefore if any man be in Christ, he is a new creature: old things are passed away; behold, all things are become new."

The words "heart" and "spirit" are used interchangeably in the scriptures. Your heart is your spirit. When the Word of God speaks about the heart of man, it is speaking of the spirit of of man. Notice that the verse we have quoted in I Thessalonians 5:23 doesn't just say "I pray God your whole heart . . ." It says, ". . . I pray God your whole spirit and soul and body . . ."

9

Referring to man's spirit, Peter talked about the "hidden man of the heart." He was telling us not merely to be concerned with outward adorning, "But let it be the hidden man of the heart, in that which is not corruptible, even the ornament of a meek and quiet spirit, which is in the sight of God of great price" (I Peter 3:4). This is the real man. It is not the outward man, the man of flesh and bones; it is not the body. It is the inward man.

Paul referred to this "hidden man of the heart" — man's spirit — as the inward man. ". . . Though our outward man perish (another version says 'is decaying'), yet the inward man is renewed day by day" (II Cor. 4:16). The outward man, or the body, is growing older and "is decaying," just as the house you live in is decaying and needs constant upkeep and repairs. But the real you is not getting older, for Paul said, ". . . yet the inward man is renewed day by day."

I will never be any older than I am right now. I am no older now than I was a few years ago. I know more now than I did then, but I'm not any older. My hair may become grayer and I may get a few more wrinkles, but the real me will never become old. For the inward man is renewed day by day.

Then Paul went on to say, "For our light affliction, which is but for a moment, worketh for us a far more exceeding and eternal weight of glory; While we look not at the things which are seen, but at the things which are not seen: for the things which are seen are temporal; but the things which are not seen are eternal" (Verses 17-18). You may be going through some kind of trial which is making your life miserable from the natural standpoint. But remember, it is just for a moment. For we look forward to something far more wonderful which will last, not for a moment, but for eternity.

"While we look not at the things which are seen, but at the things which are not seen . . ." The outward man is seen, but the inward man is that hidden, unseen man. Too many people are defeated in life because they are looking at the wrong things. All they ever see is the physical. Smith Wigglesworth once said "I'm not moved by what I see. I'm not moved by what I feel. I'm moved only by what I believe." The only way we can look at the unseen is by faith.

The first verse of the next chapter is a continuation of what Paul was saying here. When Paul wrote this epistle it was all one long letter to the church at Corinth. Man has divided it into chapters for easier reference. Talking about things that are not seen and about the inward man, Paul said, "For we know that if our earthly house of this tabernacle were dissolved, we have a building of God, an house not made with hands, eternal in the heavens" (II Cor. 5:1).

The "earthly house" that Paul talks about here is, of course our physical body. He says that if our body is "dissolved . . ." if it dies and is placed in the grave, decays and goes back to dust, that is not the end. ". . . We have a building of God, an house not made with hands, eternal in the heavens . . ." He is referring to the spirit of man, the inward man, that is eternal.

Paul continues on this subject further in this same chapter. "Therefore we are always confident, knowing that, whilst we are at home in the body, we are absent from the Lord: (For we walk by faith, not by sight:) We are confident, I say, and willing rather to be absent from the body, and to be present with the Lord" (II Cor. 5:6-8). In Verse 6 Paul said, "we are always confident;" then again in Verse 8 he said, "we are confident . . ." Paul knew what he was talking about. He was confident that while "we (the inward man) are at home in the body, we are absent from the Lord." But when we (the inward man, the real man) are "absent from the body," we are "present with the Lord."

Living in the natural, physical world as we do, it is difficult to realize that the spirit world is far more real than this natural world. We think of people as existing only in their physical bodies, and when they are dead as no longer existing. However, the scriptures tell us that the real man is the inward man, the hidden man of the heart, and he is an eternal being. He will live on long after his "earthly house" has returned to the dust.

11

Chapter III

MAN'S SECOND DIMENSION — THE SOUL

We look more closely now into the second part of man's three-fold nature — the soul. As we stated earlier, the soul is the intellect. It is man's sensibilities and will. It is the part of man that reasons and thinks. It deals with the mental realm.

In Romans 12:1 we see in Paul's teachings that we are to do something with our bodies. ". . . Present your bodies a living sacrifice, holy, acceptable unto God, which is your reasonable service." In the very next verse Paul goes on to say something about the mind, which is man's intellect, or his soul. He said that we are to do something with our mind also. "And be not conformed to this world: but be ye transformed by the renewing of your mind, that ye may prove what is that good, and acceptable, and perfect, will of God" (Verse 2).

Paul was writing here to believers. He was not writing to the heathen. He was not writing to people of the world. He was writing to born-again, Spirit-filled Christians. Yet their Christian experience had not affected their bodies or their minds. He told them that *they* were going to have to do something with their *bodies; they* were going to have to do something with their *minds.*

God isn't going to do anything with our body or our mind. God contacted our spirit. We contacted God with our spirit, and our spirit (the inward man, the hidden man of the heart) became a new man in Christ. Now it is up to us to do something. Paul said that we need to (1) do something with our bodies — "present your bodies a living sacrifice;" and (2) do something with our minds — "be ye transformed by the renewing of your mind."

One of the greatest needs of the church today is that God's people renew their minds with the Word of God. Just because a person is a Christian, and even filled with the Holy Spirit, doesn't mean that he has a renewed mind. *The mind becomes renewed with the Word of God.*

This is one reason God put teachers (those who are really called to teach) in the church — to renew our minds. Many times those who teach do so with only a natural knowledge that they have gained from the Bible and from other sources. But I am referring here to one of the ministry gifts — those who are called and anointed by the Spirit to teach.

God has given us His Word, and we can feed upon that Word. This will renew our minds. But He also put teachers in the church to renew our minds and to bring us the revelation of the knowledge of God's Word.

So our minds are renewed by two methods: (1) feeding upon God's Word in our own private study and meditation, and (2) being taught by Spirit-anointed teachers. In this way we can grow in the strength and knowledge of the Word, and can walk in its light as our minds are renewed daily with the Word of God.

Along this same line I was once asked, "Brother Hagin, how can I make my belief in God's Word more than just mental assent?"

First of all, we must understand the difference between real faith and mental assent. Mental assent agrees that the Bible is true but doesn't act on it. Real faith is acting on God's Word. Mental assent says, "I know God's Word is true all right. I know God promised me certain things and that I ought to have them." Faith sees the object of prayer as already having been attained. Faith says, "The Word of God says it, I believe it, and I have it now," even though it may not be seen in the natural. Faith says, "I have it now — not because I can see it, not because I actually possess it, but because God promised it."

"Now faith is the substance of things hoped for, the evidence of things not seen" (Heb. 11:1). Another translation of this verse reads, "Faith is giving substance to things hoped for." Our faith gives substance to it and so we can say, "It is mine."

13

Chapter IV

MAN'S THIRD DIMENSION — THE BODY

Let's look now at what the scriptures have to say about the body. As we have said, man's spirit is the *inward man,* that part of him that knows God. The body is the *outward man,* the physical, the house in which we live.

"I beseech you therefore, brethren, by the mercies of God, that ye present your bodies a living sacrifice, holy, acceptable unto God, which is your reasonable service" (Rom. 12:1). Paul was not writing to sinners here. He was writing to the saints at Rome, for he said, "I beseech you therefore, *brethren* . . ." He addresses his letter "To all that be in Rome, beloved of God, called to be saints . . . ." (Rom. 1:7). He said for us to do something with our bodies — to "present your bodies a living sacrifice . . ." It is up to us. If we don't do anything with our bodies, nothing will be done with them.

Notice also that Paul didn't say to present yourselves to God. If you are a child of God, you already belong to Him. You can't very well present to someone that which already belongs to him. You wouldn't have any right to take a handkerchief out of a man's pocket and give it to him. It already belongs to him. You cannot take a man's car out of his garage and present it to him. It already belongs to him. Neither can you take something that already belongs to God and present it to Him. It is already His.

Paul said " . . . ye (the inward man) present your bodies (the earthly house you live in) . . ." *We,* not God, are the caretaker of that house. We ourselves must present our bodies "a living sacrifice, holy, acceptable unto God, which is your reasonable service." I like another translation which says, "which is your spiritual service."

There are those who say, "Well, it doesn't make any difference about the body or what it does. This old body isn't going to heaven anyhow." But it does make a difference to God what we do with our bodies. He wants transfigured bodies. He wants us to present our bodies "a living sacrifice . . . which is your reasonable service."

Paul said, "Therefore if any man be in Christ, he is a new creature: old things are passed away; behold, all things are become new" (II Cor. 5:17). Many people are trying to get folks to join the church. They want them to do better. They want them to try to live right. But, you know, I never have tried to live right. I was just born again and I've been right ever since.

Living right is good, but it won't make you a Christian. Sitting in church on Sunday morning won't make you a Christian any more than sitting in your garage will make you an automobile. This won't take you to heaven. Being born again will, though.

Striving to be good on your own is not Christianity, it is mere religion. Christianity is being born again. Christianity is receiving the gift of eternal life. When eternal life, which is the nature and the life of God, is imparted to your spirit, it changes you. This life of God coming into man's heart makes this inward man (the real man) a new man. We don't have to make ourselves new. We couldn't anyhow. When we are born again, however, we are a new man with a new nature, for Paul said "old things are passed away (our old, sinful nature); behold, all things are become new."

After we are born again we will still have trouble with the flesh, but we won't have trouble with the real man. Some folks have said, "You have to die out to the old self." However, when we are born again the old self is already dead and we have a new self in its place. What we need to do is die out to the flesh.

But, you may say, isn't the flesh the old self? No, it isn't. Your flesh is the same body, the same flesh it was before you were saved, but that man on the inside (which was the old self, the old you) has become a new self, a new man in Christ. This inward man has become a new man. When he does, then "old things are passed away; behold, all things are become new." He is a "new creature" in Christ.

The body is not new; however, at the coming of Christ we

15

will have a new body. Right now God expects us to do something with our bodies, to present them "a living sacrifice . . ." He expects us to have control over our bodies and not let them dominate us. He does not want us to be carnal Christians, or "body-ruled" Christians. He expects us to do as Paul said in I Corinthians 9:27, "But I keep under my body, and bring it into subjection: lest that by any means, when I have preached to others, I myself should be a castaway."

Here again Paul is saying that we should do something with our bodies. He said, "*I* keep under my body . . ." *I* "bring it into subjection . . ."

Who is "I"? "I" is the man on the inside. If the body were the real you, then Paul would have said, "I keep myself under . . . I bring myself into subjection." But he didn't say that. He said, "I keep under my *body*, and bring *it* into subjection. Therefore, the "I" Paul is referring to here is the real man, the man on the inside, the hidden man of the heart, the eternal man.

Then we might ask, "Bring the body into subjection to what?" To the inward man. We don't let our body dominate us. We don't let our body rule us. We rule our body. The inward man is to rule the body.

With most folks, however, their bodies rule them. And this is what keeps them baby Christians. This is what makes carnal Christians. Earlier in this letter to the Corinthians, Paul reproved them for the fact that they were still baby Christians. Then he says, "Ye are yet carnal." In one version the word which is translated here "carnal" is translated "body-ruled." Carnal Christians are body-ruled Christians. They are letting their bodies rule them. Paul said to them, "Ye walk as mere men." In other words, they were doing things and living like people who had never been born again. They were "mere men" instead of supernaturally transformed men living victoriously in Christ Jesus.

The choice is ours. We can let our body continue to dominate us if we want. That body, if we let it, will want to go on doing the things it has always done. Or we can choose to keep our body under control. Our inward man can dominate it and present it to God, a living sacrifice.

16

Chapter V

THE HOLY SPIRIT IN THE INNER MAN

The part of man's three-fold nature that contacts God is the spirit of man. This is the real man, or as the apostle said, the inward man, the hidden man of the heart. It is the spirit of man that receives eternal life. We will have a new body one day, but we have the new life right now.

When a man is born again, eternal life is imparted to his spirit, to this inward man. "For the wages of sin is death; but the gift of God is eternal life . . . ." (Rom. 6:23). Eternal life is the life and the nature of God. It is the God kind of life. Jesus made the statement, "For as the Father hath life in himself; so hath he given to the Son to have life in himself" (John 5:26). Jesus was saying here that He, the Son, has the same kind of life that God the Father has. Then in the tenth chapter of John's gospel we read where Jesus said, ". . . I am come that they might have life, and that they might have it more abundantly" (John 10:10).

So we see that this life of God that comes into our spirits is the nature and the life of God which re-creates our spirits and makes us new creatures in Christ Jesus.

God's nature is love. Therefore, if a man is born again, he will be filled with God's love. "By this shall all men know that ye are my disciples, if ye have love one to another" (John 13:35). "We know that we have passed from death unto life, because we love the brethren. He that loveth not his brother abideth in death. Whosoever hateth his brother is a murderer: and ye know that no murderer hath eternal life abiding in him" (I John 3:14-15). John was saying here that if a man has passed from the old life, with its spiritual death, to the new eternal abundant life, he will be filled with love. If he has this eternal life in him, he will not have hate in him, he will have love.

17

The Holy Spirit is the agency that imparts eternal life to us through the Word, and through the Word conviction leads us to Christ. Then we will have a witness of the Spirit in our heart that we are the child of God (Rom. 8:16).

Although the Holy Spirit plays an important part in our regeneration, there is more to receiving the Holy Spirit than this. Afterwards the Holy Spirit will come to dwell in us as Comforter, Helper, and Guide. A woman recently told me that she had always been taught that if a person is saved he has the Holy Spirit, but that is all there is to it. He will never have any more of the Holy Spirit than he has at conversion.

It is true, as we have said, that the child of God is born of the Spirit and has the witness of the Spirit. But as we look into the book of Acts we see the apostles teaching that there is more. Philip went down to the city of Samaria and preached Christ. The people believed Philip's message concerning Jesus and the kingdom of God, and they were baptized in water. Then we read, "Now when the apostles which were at Jerusalem heard that Samaria had received the word of God, they sent unto them Peter and John: Who, when they were come down, prayed for them, that they might receive the Holy Ghost: (For as yet he was fallen upon none of them: only they were baptized in the name of the Lord Jesus)" (Acts 8:14-16).

Peter and John didn't pray that the people of Samaria might be born again. They had already received Christ as Saviour, and as Peter said, they were "born again, by the word of God, which liveth and abideth for ever."

We read then that Peter and John laid hands on these new believers and "they received the Holy Ghost" (Verse 17). So we see here that receiving the Holy Ghost is an experience subsequent to salvation.

When the Holy Spirit comes to dwell in us, He does not dwell in our heads, but in our hearts. Our head is what hinders us most of the time in receiving this experience, for the head has been used to using the tongue so much that it doesn't want to yield that tongue to the Holy Spirit. That is the reason some people struggle and struggle, trying to receive the Holy Ghost.

The only reason that our bodies become a temple of the Holy Spirit is that they are the temple, or house, of our spirit.

18

In that sense the Holy Spirit is dwelling in our body. However, the Holy Spirit is not dwelling in our body as such. He is dwelling in our spirit. ". . . Greater is he that is in you, than he that is in the world "(I John 4:4). Smith Wigglesworth said, "I'm a thousand times bigger on the inside than I am on the outside."

"And they were all filled with the Holy Ghost, and began to speak with other tongues, as the Spirit gave them utterance" (Acts 2:4). At this initial outpouring of the Holy Spirit the Bible says, "they . . . began to speak with other tongues . . ." *They* did the talking as "the Spirit gave them utterance." The real man is this inward man, and when we speak with tongues we are speaking out of our heart, out of our spirit, out of this inner man. It isn't the body speaking, even though we are using our vocal organs. And it isn't our mind. Paul said, "For if I pray in an unknown tongue, my spirit prayeth . . . ." (I Cor. 14:14).

When Jesus talked to His disciples about the promised Holy Spirit He said, "If any man thirst, let him come unto me, and drink. He that believeth on me, as the scripture hath said, out of his belly (another translation says 'his innermost being') shall flow rivers of living water. (But this spake he of the Spirit, which they that believe on him should receive: for the Holy Ghost was not yet given; because that Jesus was not yet glorified)" (John 7:37-39). Jesus was telling His disciples that the Holy Spirit would dwell in their "innermost being," in their spirit.

Therefore, we see that the Holy Spirit is not living in our head, or our minds. He is dwelling in our heart.

"But," someone might say, "I don't feel Him. Maybe He has gone away."

If He ever came, He is still there, for Jesus said, "I will pray the Father, and he shall give you another Comforter, that he may abide with you for ever" (John 14:16). This promise says nothing about staying only two weeks or a month. It says "forever." The Holy Spirit does not come and go. Once we have received Him, He will "abide with you for ever."

"But if I do wrong, won't He leave me?"

No, He won't leave you. He'll still be there trying to help you. After David had sinned by committing adultery and murder, he repented and prayed, ". . . Take not thy holy spirit from me" (Psalm 51:11). Up until that time the Holy Spirit had not left David. And He never did. We may grieve the Holy Spirit, but He will "abide with us for ever."

Because the Holy Spirit is not in our mind, He does not communicate directly with our mind. He is in our spirit and communicates with us through our spirit. Of course, our spirit does influence our intellectual process from within.

When Jesus spoke of the promised Holy Spirit He said, "Howbeit when he, the Spirit of truth, is come . . . he shall not speak of himself; but whatsoever he shall hear, that shall he speak . . . ." (John 16:13). Jesus had already stated, "I will pray the Father, and he shall give you another Comforter, that he may abide with you for ever." Then Jesus went on to say, ". . . For he dwelleth with you, and shall be in you" (John 14:17).

Jesus said that this Holy Spirit which dwells in us "shall not speak of himself; but whatsoever he shall hear, that shall he speak." Jesus said that the Holy Spirit speaks. This isn't talking about tongues. *We* talk in tongues as the Spirit gives us utterance. Jesus said that when the Holy Spirit speaks, "he will shew you things to come" (John 16:13). How is He going to do it? He is going to speak in our spirit because that is where He is. Our spirit receives information from the Holy Spirit.

The greatest things that have ever happened to me have started on the inside. That is where God starts the work. When we are saved the Holy Spirit moves on our spirit and on the inside we feel conviction. We feel the urge to respond to God. Something happens on the inside and we become acquainted with the Holy Spirit then as He speaks to our spirit.

It was on the bed of affliction that I first learned to listen to the inward voice. I didn't know how. No one taught me, I had to learn for myself. If I had started listening before I did, I wouldn't have had to stay flat on my back for sixteen months. But I didn't listen. This unseen One was trying to open the Word of God up to me, trying to get me to act on that Word, but I wouldn't do it because my natural mind wouldn't let me. It wouldn't allow me to act by faith.

I would pray and feel blessed because God will bless us when

20

we pray. But that doesn't necessarily mean we have the answer to our prayer. Too many people have based their faith on this and have been deceived when they should have been basing their faith on the Word of God.

I would check my heartbeat to see if I was healed. I would look at my poor limbs, which were wasted away, to see if I could walk. Seeing that I wasn't any better I would cry out to the Lord, "Why?"

The time came when the Holy Spirit finally got me to listen to the Word. The Spirit of God will always lead us in line with the Word. He is the Author of the written Word. Mark 11:24 was the verse of scripture that brought me off the bed of affliction. "What things soever ye desire, when ye pray, believe that ye receive them, and ye shall have them."

The Holy Spirit spoke to my heart to pay attention to the last clause in that verse — "and ye shall have them" and act as if it were true. You might say, "How did you hear the Lord?" I didn't hear any voice in the natural realm. I didn't hear anything with my physical ears. I heard it inside. I heard Him speaking indelibly to my spirit.

It is with the heart, the spirit, that man believes. It is with this inward man that we stand on God's Word, not with our head. There may be all kinds of doubts in your mind, but you believe in your heart. I had all kinds of doubts in my head, but they never hindered me. And they won't hinder you either unless you let them. It was when I obeyed that inner voice and held fast to the promise in God's Word, when I claimed my healing as an accomplished fact in spite of outward evidence to the contrary, that God delivered me from the doctor's death verdict.

The Holy Spirit can help us, can teach us and can work through us if we will just learn to be more responsive to Him. We will not learn this overnight, nor should we become discouraged when we don't. Just because you went to school one day you didn't quit, saying, "Well, I've learned it all now." You kept going and kept learning. Spiritual things come the same way. Nor will we learn without making some mistakes along the way. You didn't quit trying to drive a car just because the first time you drove you went up over the curb. You kept on until you could drive. We must keep on in our walk in the Spirit too. "Draw nigh to God, and he will draw nigh to you" (James 4:8).

It was this same inner voice that led me into the Baptism of the Holy Ghost. When I first heard someone preaching about this experience, I closed my ears to the message because I thought they were in error. Finally, the Holy Spirit, this same voice on the inside of me, spoke to my spirit, "Why don't you see what the Bible says?" He led me to passages of scripture dealing with the subject and then I accepted it. I walked in the light that the Spirit had shed in my spirit and received the Baptism of the Holy Ghost.

We read in Proverbs 20:27, "The spirit of man is the candle of the Lord, searching all the inward parts of the belly." This is saying that God uses our spirit to enlighten us, to guide and direct us. He speaks to our spirit by an inward witness. "For as many as are led by the Spirit of God, they are the sons of God" (Rom. 8:14).

Our own spirit has a voice too. We call it conscience, guidance, intuition. The world sometimes calls it a hunch. This is our own spirit talking to us. Whether a person is saved or unsaved, he is still a spirit being and can know things in his spirit. And this inward voice seeks to give guidance to our minds.

There are many, many times when if we would have followed this inward voice we could have spared ourself much heartache. If we had followed this inner witness we would never have made some of the investments which we made and lost money. If we had listened to this inner voice we would not have made some of the business deals we made and business partnerships. We would not have chosen some of the friends we did. I have seen wonderful young people who got in with the wrong crowd, chose the wrong companions, and were led away from God. There are a lot of mistakes we wouldn't have made if we had listened to the Spirit of God.

I accepted a pastor's invitation to hold a revival in his church some years ago. I didn't have a particular leading either way about the meeting, whether or not to accept the invitation. I just supposed it was all right to go there. During the revival campaign just preceding the meeting scheduled in this particular church I was praying for the evening service. While in prayer I had an inner sense that I should not go on to this next church. It was more than just a feeling. I tried to ignore it, telling myself that this would wear off. And when I got out of the Spirit it did wear off.

The next day while in prayer again, this inner voice was again present urging me not to go to that church. I couldn't understand it. I had promised the pastor I would come to his church. My word had been given, the advertising was out, and I had to go. Moreover, this was the only meeting I had scheduled I reasoned, "This is the only door that is open to me right at the moment, so I'm just going on." When I rose from my place of prayer, the inner sense left me again and I didn't give it any more thought. The next day in prayer, the Holy Spirit again urged me not to go to that church. But again I tossed the feeling aside.

When I got to this church I saw that the pastor was in trouble. I felt sorry for the congregation for a number of reasons. But I told the pastor I would go ahead and preach for him for a week as I knew questions would be raised if I left after I had been there only a few days.

Although there were several comfortable motels in the town, and although the pastor himself lived in a very nice home, he took us to the evangelist's quarters, which were little more than a chicken house out behind his house. He said, "I have quite a bit of money I need to raise in this meeting, and if we have any left over we'll give it to you. I hope we can give you $25 or $50 this week." I saw that he had planned this revival, not to get people saved, but to raise money.

I had brought my evangelistic party with me, and they had traveled 1200 miles to get there. I had to pay all their travel expenses plus my own. I paid for their meals and lodging in a comfortable motel, plus my own. And at the end of the week I received an offering of $40. I had to go to the bank and borrow $300 in order to leave town and get to my next meeting. Needless to say, this venture in failing to obey insistence of that inner voice was costly. But it was a good lesson to me.

We must learn to let our spirits dominate our minds if we are going to be successful Christians. To walk by faith means

23

to walk by the Word and to let our hearts and the inward man control us.

Some three months later I was holding a meeting and it was being greatly blessed of the Lord. Finances were very good and I was beginning to get caught up with my bills. I had a number of invitations to hold revivals immediately following this one, but I couldn't seem to get a witness on where the Lord wanted me to go. I wasn't listening for a voice. I was just waiting for a signal on the inside of me as to which invitation to accept. However, I couldn't really seem to get the go-ahead on any of them.

Time was growing short as I was in the last week of my current meeting and I knew it would be difficult to start another meeting on such short notice. There were announcements to be made and advertising to be placed in the local newspaper, etc. I said to my wife, "Well, I'd better do something. I believe I'll phone Brother So-and-so as he has asked me numerous times to come to his city for a meeting. Today is Wednesday. If I call him tonight he can place ads in tomorrow's paper and we can start our meeting next Monday night."

I went into the other room and picked up the telephone to call him. As I did, a voice on the inside of me (it wasn't a witness) startled me and I jumped. The voice said, "Don't do it. Don't do it." I had already picked up the phone, but I hadn't dialed yet. I placed the receiver back on the hook, "Lord, now what am I going to do?" I asked. "I don't have a meeting lined up for June. And I have obligations to be met. What am I going to do?"

I didn't hear any voice this time as I did before, but on the inside of me there was something that seemed to come floating up out of my inner being and say, "Just wait." This wasn't easy to do, but I knew I had heard from God, so I went back to my room.

My wife asked, "What did he say?"

"I didn't call him," I answered.

"You didn't call him? Why?"

"The Lord told me not to," I said, and she was satisfied.

The next evening we again discussed plans for our next revival meeting. I said, "Well, I have to do something, that is all there is to it. I've waited long enough. I've got to do something, for I have bills to pay." It would have been too late to begin the meeting that I had considered the night before as the deadline had passed for placing advertisements in the paper. But I thought of a pastor about 200 miles away who had asked me to come to his church anytime I could, even with only a day's advance notice.

I got up and went to call him. As I picked up the telephone and began to dial, a voice on the inside of me again said, "Don't do it."

I argued, "But Lord, what am I going to do? I've got to live. I have house payments to meet, children to feed, and bills to pay. And I don't have any foreseeable income beyond this Sunday night's offering. Surely you have somewhere You want me to go, something You want me to do."

He only answered, "Wait."

In looking to the Holy Spirit for guidance, I rely as much on what He doesn't tell me as on what He does. It is in times like these that we really learn how to trust God, to rest upon His promises and to depend completely on Him.

The Holy Spirit seemed to impress upon me to stay right where I was, that He had something good for me, and that if I left I would miss it. Then a knowledge came upon me. I couldn't tell you how I got it or how it got there. I just knew on the inside of me that the next morning the pastor was going to ask me if I could stay on for another week, which would make the fourth week of this meeting.

When I returned to the room where my wife was she asked, "What did he say?"

"I didn't call him. The Lord told me not to," I said, and she understood.

The next morning the pastor said to me, "I, uh, have something I want to ask you." He hummed and hawed a bit.

I said, "I know what it is and the answer is yes."

"Could you stay?" he asked.

"Yes, I can stay another week," I told him. And what a glorious meeting that fourth week was! The building was filled every night, souls were saved and believers were filled with the Holy Spirit.

25

One afternoon toward the end of the week the phone rang and the lady calling me said, "Brother Hagin, you may not remember me," and she told me her name. "I received the Baptism in the Holy Spirit in your meeting. The Lord has told me to give you a thousand dollars."

This is what I would have missed had I not listened to the leading of the Holy Spirit. It had been hard to wait without seeing anything, because the natural mind wants to walk by sight. But God wants us to walk by faith. Faith is of the heart. Our spirit will not be trained to walk in this way of faith overnight. We will make some mistakes along the way and miss God. But as we continue to seek after Him, we can train our spirit to be led of this inner voice.

Chapter VI

QUESTIONS AND ANSWERS

In a seminar which I recently conducted on the three dimensions of man, I devoted one entire session to answering the questions of those present. Thinking that the reader might have similar questions, I list some of the most pertinent ones here, along with my answers to them.

QUESTION: How would you describe the appearance of man's spirit?

How does it compare with his body?

Answer: We cannot measure spiritual things by physical things necessarily, and there is no particular connection between the two. The evidence of the scriptures, however, indicates that man's spiritual body is similar in appearance to his natural body.

Paul said, "I knew a man in Christ (all Bible scholars agree that he was speaking of himself) above fourteen years ago, (whether in the body, I cannot tell; or whether out of the body, I cannot tell: God knoweth;) such an one caught up to the third heaven. And I knew such a man, (whether in the body, or out of the body, I cannot tell: God knoweth;) How that he was caught up into paradise, and heard unspeakable words, which it is not lawful for a man to utter" (II Cor. 12:2-4). Paul was talking about his own experience here. He said he wasn't sure if he was in the body or out of the body. Only God knew for sure. Most theologians believe that this referred to the time when Paul was stoned and left for dead (Acts 14:19), but he got up and walked away. Most likely this is when this experience occurred. We don't have any other record of when it could have happened.

It doesn't make a great deal of difference really, but if we wanted to compare the appearance of the spirit and the body, Paul's appearance in the spiritual state was similar to his appearance in the natural. He couldn't tell that he had shrunk and become a midget. Certainly he would have known if he had. Nor did he become a giant ten feet tall in the spirit world, for he would have known that also. It would seem to me that Paul was of about the same appearance in spirit as in body.

In Luke 16:19-31 Jesus talked about the rich man and Lazarus. When Lazarus died he was carried by angels to Abraham's bosom. When the rich man died he was buried and "in hell he lift up his eyes, being in torments, and seeth Abraham afar off, and Lazarus in his bosom."

Hades, or hell, was the place of departed spirits. It was divided into two compartments. All those who were saved (in the sense that God preserved them because they had a promissory note on this) went into Abraham's bosom. Abraham was the father of the Jews.

When the rich man saw Lazarus, he recognized him. Even though this is in the spirit world, Lazarus must have looked as he did in this world or the rich man wouldn't have recognized him. He had to be about the same in the spirit world in order for the rich man to know him.

We need to realize that there is a spirit body as well as a physical body. Angels are spirits, and yet they have a form or a spirit body. God Himself is a Spirit, but that doesn't mean that He is just an influence or an intangible something as some people interpret it. He has a shape or a form, a spirit body. How do we know this? The Bible tells us that when Moses was on Mount Sinai he talked to God face to face. "Thou canst not see my face . . . ." (Exod. 33:20). Even though Moses was not allowed to look on God's face, He did have a face that could be seen. God also said to Moses, "I will put thee in a clift of the rock, and will cover thee with my hand (God must have had a hand) while I pass by: And I will take away mine hand, and thou shalt see my back parts: (He also had a back): but my face shall not be seen" (Verses 22-23).

When Peter, James and John were with Christ on the Mount of Transfiguration, they saw Moses and Elijah. If the disciples had seen these Old Testament prophets in some unusual form, they would not have recognized them. If Moses had been ten

28

feet tall, they wouldn't have known it was Moses. He would have been out of proportion.

It is not a matter of how large the spirit is any more than it is how large the brain is. The size of the human brain does not determine one's mental capacity. We all have about the same capacity. Some people are smarter than others, but this doesn't mean that the physical organ of the brain is any larger. They have just put a lot more into it.

Spiritually speaking, our spirits are born again. The spirit is the real you. The Holy Ghost comes to dwell in your spirit. Then it is according to how much you learn and develop spiritually that He can manifest Himself through you.

QUESTION: *Before the new birth, is there a spirit in man? Is the spirit renewed or re-created? The Bible says we are a new creation. Is this a re-creation?*

ANSWER: It is a new creation, but it is still a re-creation because the man is something he wasn't before.

Let's go back to the beginning, to the book of Genesis. There we see that God made man and gave him dominion over all the earth. In the beginning man's spirit, not his body, dominated him. He walked and talked with God. He was in fellowship with God. God created man for His own pleasure so He would have someone to fellowship with. When Adam sinned something happened to his spirit nature. In other words, we see the new birth in reverse. When he sinned, he didn't cease existing as a spirit being, but his spirit became separated from God and the nature of the devil came into his spirit. He became a spiritual child of the devil. Jesus said of the Pharisees, "Ye are of your father the devil, and the lusts of your father ye will do. He was a murderer from the beginning, and abode not in the truth, because there is no truth in him. When he speaketh a lie, he speaketh of his own: for he is a liar, and the father of it" (John 8:44).

This nature of the devil began to manifest itself in the human race. We see Adam's firstborn murder his secondborn and then lie about it.

This is the reason a man must be born again. This is the reason a man cannot be saved by works — he is spiritually a child of the devil. "Wherefore, as by one man sin entered into the world, and death by sin; and so death passed upon all men, for that all have sinned" (Rom. 5:12). This scripture is not talking about physical death but about spiritual death.

To understand this more fully let us read on. "For until the law sin was in the world: but sin is not imputed when there is no law. Nevertheless death reigned from Adam to Moses, even over them that had not sinned after the similitude of Adam's transgression, who is the figure of him that was to come" (Verses 13-14).

This tells us that death reigned from Adam to Moses. The Greek word for "reigned" means to reign as a king. Death reigned as a king, or had dominion over man. But there was a cessation of this death, yet people continued to die physically. The death which reigned from Adam to Moses was not physical death but spiritual death, which is separation from God. When God gave the law to Moses and set up the Levitical priesthood whereby atonement could be made for sins, then spiritual death did not reign over the people because the sin that separated them from God was atoned for. Yet they continued to die physically. Therefore, Romans 5:12-14 refers to spiritual death.

This is the reason, therefore, that man must be born again. He is separated from God and is spiritually a child of the devil. This is why someone had to pay the penalty for Adam's transgression, for man's sin, and give to man a new life — life from God. So God offers to man eternal life. "For the wages of sin is death; but the gift of God is eternal life through Jesus Christ our Lord" (Rom. 6:23). Receiving this life of God in the new birth changes our spirits. We become a new man, a new creature with the life and nature of God in us. "Therefore if any man be in Christ, he is a new creature: old things are passed away; behold, all things are become new" (II Cor. 5:17). Old things have not passed away on the outside, in the body. You have the same body you always had. But you are a new man on the inside and you must let that new man dominate you.

QUESTION: When I know things in my spirit, how do I know if they are of God?

Answer: The fact that the knowledge is of your own spirit doesn't necessarily mean that it is wrong. Many people, even those who are not Christians, know in their spirits that certain things are going to happen before they do. I have had people make

30

predictions to me and I have seen them come to pass just as they said. I am not referring here to fortune telling or crystal ball gazing.

A person can develop his own human spirit for a man is a spirit being. He can know things in his spirit simply because he is keen spiritually. People like this have learned to give heed to the voice of their own spirits. Their spirits know things that their minds do not know.

On the other hand, a child of God can also develop his spirit in spiritual things and allow the Spirit of God to show him things and tell things to him. This comes about through the study of God's Word.

Kenneth Hagin Ministries

P.O. Box 50126 • Tulsa, OK 74150-0126

Dear Friend,

We trust this book has been a blessing to you. We have endeavored to obey God and present the message He has given us in the printed word.

We are listing several books from our Faith Library which are of the same size and type as the one you have just read. God's message in them will enable the believer to fill to the utmost his place in the Body of Christ.

BOOKS BY KENNETH E. HAGIN

- **Redeemed From Poverty, Sickness, and Spiritual Death**
- **What Faith Is**
- **Seven Vital Steps To Receiving the Holy Spirit**
- **Right and Wrong Thinking**
- **Prayer Secrets**
- **How To Turn Your Faith Loose**
- **The Key to Scriptural Healing**
- **Praying To Get Results**
- **The Present-Day Ministry of Jesus Christ**
- **The Gift of Prophecy**
- **Healing Belongs to Us**
- **The Real Faith**
- **How You Can Know the Will of God**
- **The Threefold Nature of Man**
- **The Human Spirit**
- **Turning Hopeless Situations Around**
- **Casting Your Cares Upon the Lord**
- **Seven Steps for Judging Prophecy**
- **The Interceding Christian**

BOOKS BY KENNETH HAGIN JR.

- **Because of Jesus**
- **How To Make the Dream God Gave You Come True**
- **The Life of Obedience**

If you would like a complete list of all the materials available (study courses, group study books, minibooks, cassettes, etc.) please write our office and request the *Faith Library Catalog*.